John Hunter

The angels of God

And other papers

John Hunter

The angels of God
And other papers

ISBN/EAN: 9783741176326

Manufactured in Europe, USA, Canada, Australia, Japa

Cover: Foto ©Andreas Hilbeck / pixelio.de

Manufactured and distributed by brebook publishing software
(www.brebook.com)

John Hunter

The angels of God

THE ANGELS OF GOD

And Other Papers.

By John Hunter, D.D.,
Minister of Trinity Church, Glasgow.

"The real vital division of the religious part of our Protestant communities is into Christian optimists and Christian pessimists."

OLIVER WENDELL HOLMES.

LONDON: JAMES CLARKE & CO.
13 & 14, Fleet Street.   1898.

First Edition, February, 1898.

Contents.

The Angels of God.

" He shall give His angels charge over thee,
to keep thee in all thy ways. They shall bear
thee up in their hands, lest thou dash thy foot
against a stone."—PSALM XCI. 11, 12.

ANGELS may only be the creatures
of the devout imagination, yet
they are to be found in almost
every religion, in the oldest poetry,
and in the finest devotional literature of the world. Like Mel-
chizedek, they have no earthly
parentage that can be traced. The
belief in them came originally, not
out of temples, schools, and books,
but out of nature and communion
with nature, out of long and manifold contact with the marvel and
mystery of the world, and much
brooding and musing on the facts
and forces of human life. In the
poetry of all nations we find some
traces of this heavenly vision,

1

some gleams of white wings amid
the clouds and darkness round
about man and his life. The
universe in which Hebrew patriarchs and prophets and the first
Christian disciples lived and moved
was full of angels. We can as
easily think of summer without
flowers as of the Bible without
angels. They are bound up with
that poetic and religious interpretation of life which we find everywhere in the pages of the Old and
New Testaments.

There is much that is lovely and
pathetic, much deep and beautiful
meaning in this fundamental per-
suasion of humanity, and little
that is in itself unbelievable.
While we need not think of protecting and ministering angels as
we see them in pictures—delicate
and sexless creatures, with wings
and chubby faces, and large,
dreamy eyes—there is, on the other
hand, as little need to thrust aside
this ancient and almost universal

belief in races or orders of celestial
beings working silently and in-
visibly, like the hidden forces of
nature, and keeping sleepless watch
around the path of man's life upon
this earth, as a belief that does
violence to reason, or puts a strain
upon faith. A belief may be all
the more true because it appeals to
and satisfies the imagination. The
imaginative or poetic interpretation
of life must not be confounded
with the fanciful or false. It is a
superficial realism that rejects
what it cannot see and touch.
What we call our scientific and
critical methods are not the only
ways of approaching things. There
is far more in the universe than is
ever clear to the vulgar or merely
critical eye. There is no essential
antagonism between the scientific
and the poetic or religious conception of the world, but it must not
be forgotten that the scientific
view of things is only one view.
There are other and deeper aspects,

and the failure to perceive and
appreciate these may be largely due,
not so much to superior intelligence
as to spiritual defect—to the inac-
tivity or paralysis of the spiritual
imagination.   Not only through
observation and analysis, but
through imagination and feeling
and experience; not only through
the head, but through the heart
comes the great revealing and the
light of life by which we walk. We
must not allow our new studies
and new knowledge to rob us of
the vision of the world as it lies in
the imagination, and is present to
faith, or to turn our attention away
from those powers of spiritual per-
ception which to-day, as yesterday,
are the Divinest possession of our
humanity and require the largest
care and the severest culture. The
ideal may be, after all, the most
real, and insight the highest, as it
is the rarest, form of sight. We
are working toward new and finer
conceptions and expressions of the

central confidence of religion in
the livingness and beneficence of
the universe, but as yet there is no
call to cast discredit upon the way in
which our fathers expressed their
thought and trust. It is one of
the supreme offices of religion to
idealise the world and life; and a
lovelier, more illuminating, more
inspiring, more consoling vision
and interpretation of their ministries than this of angels, or one
more satisfying to the poetic and
religious feelings, it is impossible
to find.

The Biblical doctrine of angels
has reference not only to celestial
beings whose existence cannot be
proved nor disproved, but it in-
cludes all the agencies, seen and
unseen, which play a part in the
protection and development of
human life, all the influences which
guard and shape and minister to
human good. Wind and fire,
storm and pestilence, are spoken
of as the angels or messengers of

God. We find the word applied in the Old Testament to the prophets, and in the New Testament to the leaders and teachers of the early Church. Let us not put the angels too far off. What are they but our daily helpers? Nature, beauty, art, knowledge, love, joy, hardship, grief, death —are all angels, which, with faces open or veiled, may help us toward God. The subject of our meditation, then, is this larger and more practical one—the ministries of life, the powers and persons and things that are actually at work in and around our days, fulfilling the Divine purpose concerning us, caring for us with a real care and keeping us in all our ways.

1. *The Forces, Laws and Varied Influences of Nature are Angels of God.*

We must use symbols, and this

symbolism of angels is as true as
any we can find, and as helpful for
conceiving and describing those
natural powers and splendours
which form the environment of our
life. It not only invests mighty
and mysterious forces, and all
natural laws and processes with a
living glory, but it gives us a view
of things which quickens and
deepens confidence in a universe
essentially good and making for
goodness. Not only through her
sweet, serene and gracious things,
but through all her severities of
discipline nature is beneficent, or
making for beneficence. Inter-
preted in any little and literal
way, the beautiful assurances
and promises of the psalm from
which our text is taken do
not cover the facts of ˉhuman
life. We see every day that the
good man is not protected from
poison and pestilence, from cy-
clones and tidal waves, any more
than the ungodly man; that how-

ever trustful and submissive, he is
not protected from many of the
physical evils of existence, and that
amid storm and fire he is not borne
up in angels' hands in any way
that prevents suffering and death.
And yet, notwithstanding all the
dark and terrible aspects of life,
we feel that our trusts are truer
than our fears, our confidence more
in accord with universal and eternal
fact than our suspicion and scepticism, and that in some large and
comprehensive way these ancient
words of faith and hope are true,
and must be true. The real significance of things lies in their purpose and interpretation. Disen-
tangled from what is partial, and
read in the light of the chief end
of man's existence in this world,
namely, the development of his
higher life, these old sentences
have a meaning, and a deeper
meaning than can be seen on the
surface. We must seek their truth,
not in single and solitary occur-

rences and experiences, not in facts
isolated from the whole of which
they are a part, not in what we
may see here or there at any one
moment, but in the gradual development of the meaning and
final outcome of the great drama.
We must seek their truth, not in
what are called special providences
or interventions on the part of
Deity, but in the conception of a
God who not only transcends, but
resides in and acts through all the
energies and forces which we see
and know to be working in and
upon the world of nature and man,
and who in the fulfilment of His
purposes is content with long and
slow processes reaching through
centuries and ages.   The essential
and vital thing in the ninety-first
Psalm is confidence in God, confidence in His ways of working,
confidence in the beneficence of
His operations, confidence that the
dark and painful things which
beset the righteous man can do

him no real harm, cannot touch
the life in him which is life indeed,
confidence in God's ultimate protection and blessedness, that when
man seems to fall, he falls into
everlasting arms.

What a universe is this in which
we are living our little life! How
vast and awful its forces and movements, and how entirely beyond
our control! Why are we not
afraid? It is because we have
learned that God is not outside
His world; that what we call
nature is pervaded with wise and
beneficent purpose; that in all this
universe there is nought but good;
that a living Will, that is also a
good Will to every man is the
Eternal Source and Guide of the
forces which play about our life,
and that these are so ordered and
directed that they train and protect
the children of men, like angels
which have charge over us to keep
us in all our ways.

The laws of nature have often

been called merciless and cruel
because they are fixed; but in a
world designed for purposes of
discipline and for the common
good of a whole race the invaria-
bility of law is not cruelty, but
kindness—the outward and visible
sign and proof of the goodness
that is without variableness or the
shadow of a turning. We should
suffer far more from disease, storm,
and pestilence if special providences were our supreme reli-
ance. Well may Robert Browning
sing—

I have gone the whole round of creation,
I report as a man may of God's work,
All's love, yet all's law.

The forces and laws of nature,
pitiless though they sometimes
appear, are yet our friends and
teachers. When we put ourselves
in line with them they serve us
like angels, yield us all their
strength, and bear us up in their
hands. The conditions of our life

with nature are in many respects
hard, but wisely and mercifully so.
We are here to be educated. Out
of man's tragic struggle with
nature civilisation has grown.
Accidents, disasters, calamities
have helped to develop the noblest
qualities of our humanity. The
severities of the universe are the
severities of love, after all—the
heavenly Father training His
earthly children. The Hebrew
poet was right when he spoke of
winds and flaming fires as angels
of the most High. O blessed soul,
that has such a sublime confidence!

But the ministry of nature is
not all of a severe character. It is
often gentle and bright, ministering by means of its bounty and
beauty to human growth, human
culture, human joy. What angels
of healing hide in the sunbeams!
What vital forces reside in air and
water! What gracious work they
do in building up and nourishing

our life! There is a deep truth in Landor's line—

We are what suns and winds and water make us.

When we muse on the enrichment and enlargement of life, the strength and peace which have come from the sights and sounds of the natural world, from dawn and sunset, from shining noonday heavens and the mystery of night, from deep woods, rushing rivers, far-spreading lakes and great seas, from the beauty of the hills and the majesty of the high mountains, how else can we think of these natural influences but as angels of God charged to bless us and keep us in all our ways.

2. *The Angels of Love and Friendship.*

But turn now from nature to man, and think what angels of God our fellow-beings are to us. Helpful human beings are the chief instruments of the eternal Goodness and Care. They are none the less angels because they are clothed with flesh and blood, have features often rugged, and are not quite free from the failings of humanity. In the Gospels we read that angels ministered unto Jesus, but the little children who brightened a dark and troubled hour of His mortal day, and the women who gave Him their love, the service of their hands, their precious ointment, their tears, were as truly angels in His sorrowful and lonely life as those which, we are told, found Him wandering in the wilderness and fainting in the garden. We speak of earthly and heavenly, human and Divine love, as if all true love were not heavenly and Divine! In human love and care we see the Divine love and care. Many a poor soul to whom the Eternal Goodness was a mere abstraction has found in the love of fatherhood, or motherhood, or wifehood, or sisterhood, the messenger and revelation of the heavenly love, the mediator and interpreter of the Divine charity. Love in man's heart or woman's heart comes from God, and leads back to God. In Raphael's great masterpiece, the " Sistine Madonna," in the Dresden gallery, we see, clothed in almost spiritual tints, the angel aspect of motherhood. What may be so helpful, so full of moral protection and inspiration as a mother's love? And how full a true and noble friendship is of the highest helpfulness! how it protects against passing weakness and discouragement and keeps one loyal to what is best! Its influence always tends to idealise life. "You were an angel to me," wrote Carlyle to Emerson, "and absorbed in the beautifullest manner all thunderclouds in the depths of your immeasureable ether." "Our friends," Emerson himself said, "are those who make us do what we can."

How often have little children been to men and women as angels of God, softening their hardness, protecting and strengthening the good in their natures, and restraining and destroying the evil! Very beautiful are the words with which George Eliot closes one of the chapters in "Silas Marner."

"In the olden days there were angels who came and took men by the hand and led them away from the city of destruction. We see no white-winged angels now; but yet men are led away from threatening destruction—a hand is put into theirs, which leads them forth gently toward a calm and bright land, so that they look no more backward, and the hand may be a little child's."

Every man has his guardian angel. It may be a parent whose love never faints; it may be a wife who bravely bears and hides the

infirmities and sins of her husband ;
it may be a little child that softens
the heart growing hard in the
struggle of life ; it may be a sister
moving in thoughtful and self-
denying ways around a careless
brother, and whose love outlasts
many an affection that seems for a
time more ardent ; it may be a
noble and faithful friend that keeps
one true to his better self ; it may
be the constant example of a good
man, who carries wherever he goes
the atmosphere of a higher world ;
it may be a poet, a prophet, a
teacher whose words inspire faith
and kindle hope. Angels every
one, protecting, directing, strengthening, inspiring us, bearing us up
in their hands, and leading and
keeping us in the beautiful ways of
God ! Angels, alas ! we often only
see and know them to be when the
clouds are receiving them out of
our mortal sight for ever.

And what are our dead, what
the memories they leave behind,

what their spiritual influence, but
a part of the ministry of life;
angels of God who protect us from
evil and stimulate us to do good,
deliver us from ignoble moods,
keep us true to high ideals and
aims, a safeguard and inspiration
in hours of critical strain and trial?
Death has, indeed, its gracious com-
pensations.   How it hallows life!
Our heavenly friends, from what
may they not save us, and to what
may they not urge and lead us?

> Hand in hand with angels,
>   Through the world we go;
> Brighter eyes are on us
>   Than we blind ones know.

3. *The Angels of Daily Duty and Discipline.*

What a good angel is work—the
daily task from whose pressure we
cannot escape ! What low thinking
is that which calls labour a 'degra-
dation!' It may sometimes take
the form of rude and grinding toil,
but even then it has a blessing in

it. It is an angel of God, even though it may be clad in mean and rough garments. Goethe saves his fallen Faust through honest and hard work, and at every step it makes him nobler and better. Prayer is a vital necessity of all deep and earnest life, but work is as needful as prayer, simply as a means of moral protection. It is an angel of God, not only by what it guards us from, but by what it leads us to. It is a potent means of education, and the secret source of much of the energy and wisdom and goodness which bless the world. Often, too, the best help and comfort that can be found in sorrow is found in the daily duty, in doing what has to be done. It saves one from many morbid thoughts and cravings, and from the isolation and selfishness of grief.

4. *The Angel of Trial and Death.*

Shall we call pain and grief, disappointment, bereavement, loss,

failure, the penalties of wrong-
doing, sickness and death, angels
of God? Why not? We cannot,
of course, put them among the
angelic band if comfort and ease
be regarded as the ideal and end
of life. But if strength and forti-
tnde, submission and patience,
wisdom and sympathy be the
greatest blessings of life and its
crown of rejoicing, then we must
call our sorrowful experiences
angels of God, part of a beneficent
and Divine ministry. Not only
the fair and gracious things which
sweeten and gladden our days, but
the calamities which sweep away
our happiness, the winds which
break our hopes, the storms which
smite our hearts and empty our
lives are the messengers which
fulfil God's word, and have received
a charge concerning us to bear us
up in their hands, lest we grow
superficial and light - minded,
worldly and proud. In our path
through life much hath been

grievous to flesh and blood, and
doubtless much shall still be——
but what then?

Who is the angel that cometh?
       Pain!
Let us arise and go forth to greet him;
       Not in vain
Is the summons come for us to meet
    him;
       He will stay
And darken our sun;
       He will stay
A desolate night, a weary day.
Since in that shadow our work is done,
And in that shadow our crowns are won,
Let us say still, while his bitter chalice
Slowly into our hearts is poured,—
Blessed is he that cometh
In the name of the Lord.

A life unvisited by the angel of
sorrow is apt to be a life without
thought, a life without pathos, a
life without depth, a hollow and
petty life, a hard and fruitless
life. Let us meet our sorrow
when it comes in the right
spirit, and not as spoiled children,
and it will work for our good,
and we shall win from it a

blessing. It is the paradox of Christianity that out of poverty we are made rich, out of weakness we are made strong, that we lose to gain, and die to live.

And what are the penalties that follow our transgressions? When men truly understand what moral law means and moral life, they will also understand that the sternest penalties of their wrongdoing, and not the things which ward them off, are the angels of God.

So by our woes to be,
Nearer, O God, to Thee.

And what about Death? We have called it by many hard names —the Great Destroyer, the King of Terrors, and such like. One does not like to think of the fear which in the popular mind is associated with death. It is due to ignorance and superstition, or to the effeminacy which is born of the soft indulgences of life.

Let us look for the angel-aspects

of death, for they are many. To
one who believes in Eternal Goodness at the heart of things, it must
be unquestionable that whatever
is inevitable and universal must
also be beneficent. When we
look at nature we find that the
things which are common are all
good; and death when it comes,
not prematurely, but naturally, is
no exception to the rule. It is
chiefly by the survivors the pain
and sorrow of it are felt. Even
when the transition seems violent,
it is not so violent as it seems to
the onlooker. When shall we give
to this angel of God the name
which Jesus gave it? When shall
we be able to use in a real, and not
in a mechanical and conventional
way the great words struck out in
the first exultation of the Christian
faith—Death is abolished! Death
is swallowed up by Victory!

Who is the angel that cometh?
Death!
But do not shudder and do not fear;

He comes to help and to save and to
      heal,
    Blessed is he that cometh
    In the name of the Lord.

5. *The Angels of Inspiration.*

Let us not overlook among the
celestial ministries what may be
called the angels of inspiration—
the inspiration which created our
Sacred Scriptures, and which fills
onr minds and souls to-day with
heavenly visions and voices. What
are our serious impressions and
profound convictions, what our
gleams of insight, what our touches
of finer feeling, what our nobler
impulses, what our longings and
aspirations, what those formless
visions that sometimes illuminate
our days, what those unvoiced
words which we have heard again
and again amid the silence of the
hills, under the midnight stars, by
the wayside of quiet meditation,
in moments of trial when we have
been deeply moved? What are

they all but the visitations of the
living God? The old Hebrew
would have described them as the
angels of God coming to him, and
the angels of God speaking to him.
Heaven and God are not farther
away from us than they were from
the patriarchs and apostles. The
stories of open heavens, of descend-
ing and ascending angels, of
spiritual voices, and suchlike, are
not merely the records of an
ancient, but vanished experience.
We too are God's children. We
too are susceptible to spiritual
impressions because we ourselves
are spirits. The days of inspiration
are not over. The Angels of God
are ever with us. They haunt us
at every turning. Do not be indifferent to their presence! Do
not think them absent because you
cannot catch the expression of their
face, or trace the outlines of their
form. The spiritual presences are
the most real presences. Let not
the ministries of life and death, of

the visible and invisible world be
lost upon you. In God's good
Name, I plead with you to welcome
the heavenly messengers.

Around your lifetime golden ladder
    rise ;
And up and down the skies
With winged sandals shod
The angels come and go, the messengers
    of God.

Our Sources of Refreshment and Renewal.

*" He shall drink of the brook in the way;
therefore shall he lift up the head."*
                                    PSALM CX. 7.

TRADITION has ascribed this psalm
to David, but it is, perhaps, better
understood when we read it as the
production of one of David's
devoted followers. To treat it as
one of the Messianic psalms, and
believe that it finds a certain true
and large fulfilment in Jesus
Christ, we are not required to
ignore or deny its basis of con-
temporary fact. The higher reaches
of the human imagination are
ever full of prophecy, and no
prophecy of Scripture, we are told,
is of private or particular interpretation.

In the latter part of the psalm

the king is represented as engaged
in conflict. At a wayside stream
he quenches his thirst, and is thus
enabled with revived ardour to
continue the pursuit of the enemy.
"He shall drink of the brook in
the way; therefore shall he lift up
the head." In the olden days of
warfare and trouble what a thing
of beauty and blessing was the
brook by the way! And to-day, as
yesterday, it is a true and lovely
symbol of all those influences,
natural and spiritual, which refresh and renew the inner life.

In this strange pilgrimage that
we call human life what traveller
does not sigh now and again, for
the brook by the way? The great
human necessities are not confined
to any condition or time, yet it
would seem that never, as now, was
there such need of the influences
which refresh and restore. How
restless and intense our life! How
killing the pace! How constant
and keen the conflict! How many

temptations to forget the early dream and inspiration, and to let the fine power and ardour of youth waste away into vulgar prudence! How soon we begin to mourn over the fading of enthusiasm, even in the best work, and the loss of freshness of spirit in dealing with the duties involved in the manifold relations of life. How much there is around us, not only to quicken thought, but to dissipate it; not only to arouse energy, but to exhaust it! There are special seasons also of strain and trial, when zest and zeal pass away, and duty wears the forbidding look of drudgery, and we walk slowly and wearily where once we marched swiftly and full of hope.

Brooks by the way! The heart asks for them, and the God in whom we trust, the Shepherd of our pilgrimage, has placed them within our reach. The wilderness of our discipline is not a dry and waste howling one. It has its Elims, as

well as its Marahs, its green pas-
tures and quiet waters, as well as
its valleys of the shadow of death.
How they abound, these springs
and streams of refreshment, these
good and gracious influences which
take the fever and fret out of the
heart, restore the soul, renew the
beauty and joy of life, and make
us feel in every part of our being
the healing touch of the Infinite
Strength and Peace!

(1) In one of his letters, Na-
thaniel Hawthorne speaks about
bathing himself in "the refreshing
waters of solitude and open-air
nature," and there is no season of
the year in which we may not find
this source of rest and refreshment
for the mind and heart. The Creation may always be our recreation.
To be in love with this beautiful
world is to be at the secret source
of many a noble pleasure. To have
a mind and heart open to the highest impressions of the natural universe, to be able to enter into the

life of a summer or winter day, to
enjoy a night of stars, to feel the
beauty of a flower, the grandeur of
a storm, the spell of the wide waters
or the high mountains is to have
abundant means of recovery and
renewal always nigh at hand when-
ever we feel the need of calling
ourselves off for awhile from the
excitement and strain of the daily
conflict. It is true, nature does
not yield the sympathy which the
passionate human heart requires,
but insensibly she helps her lovers
to bear their burdens and to find
rest in God. We are quickened
and comforted by outward things
more than we know. The sun
and moon and stars, unaffected by
our little controversies, rebuke and
soothe us as we gaze on their tranquil glory. The mountains bring
peace, and our fretfulness is carried
away by the rushing river at our
feet. Not only in the synagogue
did Jesus find refreshment, but
in the lilies of the field, in the

sunset sky, among the hills, and
by the lake of Galilee. In his
suggestive journal, Amiel, describing a country walk taken when a
dark and troubled mood was upon
him, thus writes: "The sunlight,
the green leaves, the sky, all
whispered to me, ' Be of good
cheer and courage, poor wounded
one!' " We are all at times poor
wounded ones, needing all the
refreshment and healing we can
find. And,

What simple joys from simple sources
    spring!

The quiet ministry of nature,
the play of natural influences upon
us, may be full of renewing grace.
Beyond the satisfaction of taste
and sentiment, this experience
which we call contact and communion with nature may be a gain
to the whole spiritual being;
soothing and relieving mental pain,
quickening a more hopeful spirit,
nourishing all finer feelings, and,

like every deep human experience,
taking the soul into the presence
of the Eternal.

Let us make the most and the
best of this source of refreshment
and renewal. We are sent into
the world, not only to solve its
problems, fight its battles, and put
away its sin by the sacrifice of
ourselves, but to find joy and rest ;
and through rest and joy, the
deepening and enlargement of our
life. There is a religious as well
as an irreligious worldliness. "All
things are yours, . . . the world
. . . and things present."

(2) In the familiar saying of
Herder, in his last illness : "Give
me a great thought, that I may
refresh myself with it," we find
the suggestion of a second source
of refreshment and renewal. We
have at our constant command the
greatest thought, the highest wisdom, the finest feeling of the
teachers and leaders of mankind.
The world's best literature abounds

3

with thoughts that are full of pure
refreshment and healing life. If
the supreme test of inspiration be
the power to inspire, then, how
many inspiring books it is, or may
be, our privilege to know—books
which transfigure the world to our
thought, give a noble and divine
interpretation to life, furnish the
mind with new interests, refresh
and renew the heart, and are an
open road to the purest and most
enduring of earthly enjoyments.
The joy which Longfellow said he
found in the sympathetic study of
Dante is within reach of all.
Almost any day and hour we may
leave the hot and dusty highway
and the field of contention for the
peace and freshness of some great
book that ministers to all that is
best in us. Why should life be the
dry and thirsty land it is to so many,
when all around us in shining garments stand the poets and prophets of God, waiting to lead us
to fountains of living waters?

(3) In the first book of Samuel we read, " When the evil spirit was upon Saul, David took an harp and played with his hand : so Saul was refreshed, and was well." Not only literature, but all true and noble art may be an influence that soothes the healthy, as well as the sick and morbid mind, and be, not only the opiate, which, alas! it too often is, that induces a base forgetfulness, but a pure and blessed source of refreshment to earnest souls. What wonderful power music and song, eloquence and painting, have always had to move the souls of men! By ministering to the higher nature they reinforce mind and body, and by quickening the spiritual imagination remand much of what would otherwise disquiet and dishearten to its own obscurity and insignificance. There is no more desirable a thing than a good hobby. The violin and organ, for instance, have been to many a

brook in the way that has refreshed and nourished an ideal life.

(4) Let a sentence from George
Macdonald point out another river
of the water of life at which we
may often drink and be refreshed:
"To know a man who can be
trusted will do more for one's
moral nature than all the books of
divinity that were ever written."
The beauty of the outward world
is full of divine help, but there is
more beauty and more inspiration
in living excellence than in the
fairest natural scenes. Wonder-
fully refreshing is the heart's
speech of the truly wise and good,
but more beneficent is the brave
thought when it becomes the
brave deed, and more life-giving
the Divine Word when it is made
flesh and dwells among us. How
rich the quickening and renewing
influences which come from the
presence and example of men who
lift clearly before us the nobler
ideals of life; from the memory of

the faithful dead; and from the
biographic page—

Bright affluent spirits, breathing but to
    bless,
Whose presence cheers men's eyes and
    warms their hearts,
Whose lavish goodness this old world
    renews,
Like the free sunshine and the liberal air.

Blessed beyond all price is the
friendship that stimulates us to do
our best, that is potent to dispel
morbid broodings, to cheer and
brighten life, and that helps us
even by its unconscious influence
to look at things in a larger and
better way. And here we find
the truest use of the study of
biography. Every good and faithful life with which we become
acquainted is a positive addition to
our moral power, to those influences which in days of depres-
sion, when stupor creeps over
us and weariness, revive hope and
arouse energy.

(5) The wise and religious

culture of the home affections will disclose many brooks by the way, full of the very water of life that flows from the throne and heart of God. When the Heavenly Father ordained that we should live in families, He placed within our reach sources of happiness and strength that from age to age have been as springs in the desert. It is in the home we must seek to cherish and renew our best life. We are far from having exhausted its possibilities. We lose much that is refreshing indeed if we neglect to cultivate its quiet and simple pleasures. The late John Richard Green wrote, just before his death—" What seems to me to grow fairer as life goes by is the love and tenderness of it, the laughter of little children, and the simple talk by the fireside."

(6) "What do we live for, if not to make life less difficult for each other?" is a saying of George Eliot's that indicates

another pure and unfailing source
of refreshment and renewal. Sympathy gives us new interests. It
is impossible to feel life dull and
vacant if we fill it with unselfish
cares and helpful activities. We
must have our share of the sorrow
and bitterness of life, and grow
familiar with the pain of sacrifice.
It is a discipline we cannot spare,
if we would be perfect. But in
our darkest and most depressed
hours there is always one source
of comfort nigh at hand—we can
do somethng for others. There
may be seasons when we cannot
find help for ourselves, but there
is no season when we cannot give
help. And this giving of help
will, in due time, bring its reward.
Soon shall we prove, in our own
experience, the truth of the
Saviour's word, "It is more
blessed to give than to receive."

(7) "There is a river, the
streams whereof shall make glad
the city of God, the holy place of

the tabernacles of the Most High."
We must seek, as our fathers did,
the perennial springs of refreshment that are to be found in the
private and public ordinances of
religion. The excitements and ex-
haustions of modern life make
this duty even more imperative.
Industry and enterprise are good;
but life is not only action, it is
thought and feeling also. We do
ourselves the greatest wrong, if we
allow our activities to crowd
meditation and prayer out of our
days and to rob us of the secret of
rest in God. To have depth and
elevation and tranquillity in life,
and the aim kept high and the
impulse true and steady, it is
absolutely necessary for mind and
heart to have constant access to
the Source of inspiration. It is
a moral calamity to lose the
meditative and worshipful spirit.
Reverence, faith, and aspiration
are the springs of noble and fruitful living. Sunday and the Church

stand for our highest life. They invite us to drink of waters that rise from cool and unpolluted depths. They offer an opportunity of finding that truest rest and recreation which come through mental and spiritual quickening and uplifting, and of verifying the word of prophecy, "They who wait on the Lord shall renew their strength."

(8) "Come unto Me all ye that labour and are heavy laden, and I will give you rest. Take My yoke upon you and learn of Me, for I am meek and lowly in heart; and ye shall find rest unto your souls." This invitation, so large and sweet and tender, and which needs to be made clear and impressive to each succeeding generation, is an invitation to seek refreshment and renewal through trust and obedience. In the fellowship of Jesus Christ we lose our ignorant and guilty fears, and our selfish and vexing cares; we find a heavenly Father, we learn to take a gracious view

of life, even of its hardest circumstances, and to be at peace with things; we come to love the will of God, and to rejoice in the good of others as if it were our own; we enter into the Saviour's sense of immortality, and are persuaded that in the body and out of the body we are compassed about by the atmosphere of Infinite Love. What can refresh the weary heart and life like the spiritual persuasions, the great trusts and hopes which are the secret of Jesus, and which He communicates to all who put themselves under His influence, and seek to live in the communion of His Spirit? How the words spoken more than nineteen centuries ago near Jacob's well interpret our spiritual experience to-day! "Whosoever drinketh of the water I shall give him shall never thirst; but the water I shall give him shall be in him a well of water springing up unto eternal life."

Belief and Life.

" Lord, I believe ; help Thou mine unbelief."
ST. MARK IX. 24.

THE state of mind which the Evangelist Mark ascribes to the father of the lunatic child is not uncommon. His broken confession and appeal, " Lord, I believe; help Thou mine unbelief," indicate the condition of many. They believe, and they do not believe.

Light half-believers of our casual creeds,
  Who never deeply felt, nor clearly willed,
Whose insight never has borne fruit in deeds.

To realise the meaning of truths we do not doubt, and, perhaps, never dream of doubting; to think more deeply what we think; to feel more deeply what we feel; to have a real and living belief in the high and solemn things we say we believe—this is what nearly all of us, brought up in Christian homes and churches, most need.

The temptations to scepticism and unbelief which approach men through the inquiring and critical intellect assail only the few. And in the life, sensitive and loyal to pure moral ideals, they will not long weaken and hinder. The just live by faith, and can find no abiding satisfaction in negation or doubt. The obedient spirit will not be left to wander in darkness; the servant faithful over a few things will not miss at last the joy of the Lord; and to the pure in heart will be given, as of old, that vision of God which is the crown of life.

But we must be cheated by mere words, names and professions, if we fail to see that the unbelief which assails the vast mass of men and women is not intellectual, and cannot be removed by any intellectual process. What we have most

to fear in these, as in all days, is a
faith not alive, or only half alive ;
a belief that is not a spiritual conviction and experience, that is not
taken into the heart, and therefore
never works any change in affection and motive, in character and
life. Belief and life, etymologists
tell us, spring from the same root.
Of this we may be sure, that we
never truly believe anything until
such a belief produces its natural
result in the life. There is no true
believing when we profess one
thing and live and act in a con-
trary way. To believe truly is to
live truly, and the faith that
justifies and saves contains "the
promise and potency" of all righteousness. Men often measure their
belief, not by its quality, nor by its
power over them, but by the
number of articles to which they
give their assent. It is a word-
faith, not a heart-faith. Now a
belief in many things is of little or
no value, if it is only faint and

formal belief. Strength and
beauty and fruitfulness of life
depend, not on how many things
we believe, but on how much we
believe in anything. Our supreme
need is, not more articles of belief,
but more real believing of what we
say we believe.

(1) "I believe in God." What
a majestic affirmation that is, and
how much it comprehends! It is
a confession which touches the
beginning and the end of human
faith. It is the first and the last
word of religion. Jesus Christ
lived and died to bring us to God,
and His work and joy will be fulfilled when God is all in all to His
children.

How often we say, "I believe
in God!" How easily the sentence
falls from the lips! But it is one
thing to say it, and another thing
to live as one who feels God to be
the Alone and Everlasting Reality
of human life. "I believe in
God." Yes, but with what sort of a

belief? "Thou believest there is
one God," writes St. James with
solemn sarcasm; "thou doest well;
the devils also believe." Mr.
Froude says of Sir Robert Cecil
that he believed in God in "a
commonplace kind of way." When
a man says, "I believe in God,"
the question is, What is the quality
of his belief and what its influence?
Does he hold the belief, or does
the belief also hold him? The
selfish man who has lost all sense
of the eternal necessity for truth
and righteousness of life, says, "I
believe in God," but his belief is
not worth anything. In his business and intercourse with men he
lives "without God;" he is ruled
and guided, not by the Divine will,
but by passion, pride, pleasure,
self-interest.

Atheism of thought need not
trouble us much. Few persons
entertain it with serious consist-
ency. "Man," says the poet,
"cannot be God's outlaw, even if

he would." We cannot guard our
unbelief. All the deeper movements and experiences of life are
constantly forcing us out of it.
The atheism we have most to fear
is something infinitely more subtle
and dangerous than any theory or
definition, however negative, of the
mystery of the universe. The
worst atheism is practical, not
theoretical. It is atheism of feeling and atheism of conduct—
feeling and acting as if there were
no God, no Eternal Righteousness,
no Eternal Love; as if the relations of life had no divine order,
and the events of life no divine
significance. He is not altogether
"without God," who is loyal to his
ideal of the highest and best.
"To do justice and judgment, is
not this to know Me? saith the
Lord." But there is no such atheist
as the man who sneers in his heart
when he is reminded of principle
and duty; who allows selfish passions to obscure and distort his

moral vision, and to whom in daily
life private gain or pleasure is
more than aught besides. Much
conventional belief in God must be
as little pleasing to Him as unbelief. It is unbelief. To act as
if it were safer at any time to do
wrong than right, to follow lies
than truth—that is the worst way
of denying God. It is not possible
for us to believe truly in "God the
Father Almighty," and yet not be
different in behaviour and spirit in
every relation and experience of
life from what we would be if we
did not believe in God. To believe
truly in God is to believe in the
things which constitute the character and will of God. To believe
in God is to believe in truth,
righteousness, mercy, and love, as
principles to be carried out to the
utmost extent, and to be trusted
and followed in the direst ex-
tremity. To believe in God is to
maintain the trustful and hopeful
temper amid all the troubles of

4

life, because the experiences of
these passing days lie under the
shadow of the Great White Throne,
and are part of the heavenly
Father's education of His children.
It may not be required of us to
put our faith into words, but if it
is a real and living faith in God it
will be known and read of men in
the righteousness, the unselfish-
ness, the charity, the faithfulness,
the hopefulness, the divine beauty
of the life.

(2) We believe in Jesus Christ
the Son of God. It is the meaning
of the Christian revelation that
God was in Christ reconciling the
world to Himself; that being
infinite in love and sympathy He
bears on His heart the sorrow and
sin of mankind, and that Christ
reveals Him bearing them—reveals
the Eternal Passion and Sacrifice.
In Christ the Divine Goodness is
not only taught, but incarnate.
God in Christ is, in truth, Christianity. How few realise this

belief! The average religious man
is more Pagan than Christian in
his conception of the Divine
character and ways. We say we
believe in the Deity of Jesus
Christ, but do we not miss altogether and fail to realise the vital
spiritual truth of the doctrine
when we think of the Invisible
God as having dispositions toward
His creatures and His children that
are not Christ-like; when we think
that God can be less or other than
that which the Son reveals Him to
be, less than infinite in His com-
passion and helpfulness, other than
the Everlasting Father and Saviour
of men? "The love of God in
Jesus Christ our Lord" is the
heart of the Christian Gospel. Do
we believe it? It is true that the
presence and spirit of Christ in
human life quicken and deepen the
sense of sin, but it is also true
that in the circle of Christ's influence and in His fellowship, the
liveliest and deepest sense of sin

can never lead to despair. The
man who truly believes in Jesus
Christ, the Son of God, believes in
redeeming mercy and grace; he is
delivered from the fear which
weakens and the despair which
kills; dark regrets and forebodings
are no longer his companions, the
gloom and anguish and dread
have gone out of his soul; he is
more than conqueror, "through
Him that loved us," over all the
shadows and spectres of evil which
once pursued and vexed him.

But Jesus Christ is also the
realisation and revelation of the
Divine ideal of our human righteousness and the manifestation of
its possibility to our doubting
souls. He stands for a distinct
order of character and life. In
Him we know man to be the Son
of God and the brother of His
fellow-man. To believe in Him is
to believe in ourselves. He is
ourselves in prophecy and antici-
pation; the type and promise of

the perfection possible to every one
of us. "I believe in Christ," we
say; but what is the belief worth
in the way of the great endeavour
to be conformed to the image of
His holy living and dying? We
must not imagine we are truly
believing in Him if we are allowing a spirit that is the foe of His
spirit to move and rule us, and to
hinder us, perhaps, from even
trying to obey the heavenly vision.
To believe in Christ is to be set
free from selfish passions; it is to
be filled with His enthusiasm for
the will of God and the service of
mankind, with the spirit of His
obedience unto death and the
charity of His Cross. Has the
Lord and Saviour of men any such
believers, any such companions in
His filial devotion and sacrifice?
Good Christians we think ourselves
to be, but do we follow Christ?

(3.) We believe in the Holy
Spirit; believe that there is a
Spirit of truth and holiness and

love, and that this Spirit is God's Spirit and is present in our nature and life. We believe this, and yet we do not allow our belief to produce its proper result. We do not surrender ourselves to the guidance of the Spirit, and strive with our might to bring our inward and outward life into conformity, that the one may not put the other to a secret or open shame. We allow vulgar passion and desire to subdue and silence the Divine pleading within us. Day after day we follow our selfish inclinations and refuse to be led by the Holy Spirit of God.

"Father, Son, and Holy Spirit." It is easy to repeat this ancient confession of faith, but are we living in the reality of that which we acknowledge to be true? It is easy to repeat phrases and to quote texts. It is easy to imagine that we are "in the faith," because we think this and that about the faith. The confession God wants

is that of the heart and life, and
all other confession is only good
as it is a means to this end. To
believe truly in the Father is to be
living as faithful children; to
believe truly in the Son is to be
arming ourselves with the same
mind; and to believe truly in the
Spirit is to be obedient in word
and deed to our heavenly visions
and persuasions.

Not only from heresy and false
doctrine, but from make-believe
belief and from all barren and
dead faith, we must ever pray God
to deliver us. Lord, we believe!
believe in the great revealing
moments of existence, when the
spells of custom and the world are
broken, and we stand nearest
Thee; but when we tread again
the common levels of life, and are
tempted to forget, yea, to deny the
heavenly vision and voice, Help
Thou our unbelief.

The Power to be Quiet.

"UNQUIETNESS," says an old writer, "is the greatest evil that can come into the soul except sin." The truth and force of this remark will be seen when we consider a few of the blessings which depend on the power to be quiet.

(1) Consider how much we lose of the beauty of the world when our hearts are full of the unrest which selfish desire and striving generate. Without the tranquil mind it is almost impossible to enjoy nature, and quite impossible to hear its pensive undertones. The flowers, and hills, and stars, the running brooks, and the winds among the trees tell us little, if anything, of their secrets when we are disquieting ourselves in vain. We must be quiet to get

the best impressions from this universe of sights and sounds.

(2) Consider how much we lose of what is gracious, beautiful, and helpful in our human relations, because we carry about with us an unquiet mind, a heart seldom or never

> At leisure from itself
> To soothe and sympathise.

Our restless and selfish moods, tempers, and habits diminish our sensitiveness to the poetry and pathos of human life, take from us the gift of appreciation, and leave us with little power to respond to the sweet and gentle sanctities of home and friendship.

(3) Consider how much we lose of ourselves, how we fail to come into true and complete possession of ourselves, because we have so little of the power to be quiet. The literary sense, one of the masters of literature tells us, perishes for want of repose, and

the same might be said of even finer
and more precious gifts—the gifts
which make of men great prophets
and great saints. Alas! for all
that God gives and man loses.

(4) The power to be quiet has
its intellectual value. It is necessary to clear, deep, and strong
thinking. The mind must be
quiet to get the best work out of
itself, and to be able to penetrate
or grasp clearly any subject.
Vexed by vulgar desires or irritated
by slights, it cannot secure that
concentration of power which is so
essential to clearness and direct-
ness of vision. To think to any
good purpose it is not enough even
to be alone; we must have the
power to be quiet when we are
alone—the power, that is, to hold
the mind calmly and steadily to its
work above all the strife and
tumult of the lower life.

(5) The power to be quiet has
its ethical as well as its purely
intellectual value. To be able to

answer in moments of critical trial the vital question, " What is the right thing to do? what is my duty?" we must be able to separate ourselves from the excitement and urgent pleading of private desire and interest, and from the tyranny of worldly idea and custom, from the convention which often takes the place of conscience. The clear vision only comes to the calm heart—the heart free from wrong feeling and selfish affection. It is the placid lake that reflects the mountains and the blue skies, and, when the night comes down, the everlasting stars. So it is in the quiet soul the lights of the moral heavens reflect themselves.

(6) To receive the deepest religious impressions, to have the great truths of religion as a real and vital possession, we must have the power to be quiet. The eternal voices are not heard when the world and passion are speaking, and we are troubled about many

things. The visions of the seer
and mystic ask for discipline and
quietude. It is the calm, brooding
spirit that has given us the
prophets of the East and the
West. The quiet and contemplative mind shares the blessing
of the pure in heart ·who see God.
"Be still and know." "When I
was silent I heard a voice." It is
in stillness and silence, when mind
and heart and soul are fully awake
but calm, that we are most conscious of the One Presence.

In secret silence of the mind
My heaven and there my God I find.

Many of us find it hard to believe
what we would fain believe, and
much of our religion is a dim and
doubtful tradition, just because we
have lost the power to be quiet.
Out of life and experience come
the great revealings. "What
does it matter," as George Fox
once said to Cromwell, "that we
have the Scriptures if we have lost

the Spirit that wrote them?"
We cannot expect the unseen
things to be supreme and commanding realities to us if they are
never allowed to get sole and
undisturbed possession of our feeling and thought, and if all those
secret and subtle ways are closed
by which the Silent Spirit ap-
proaches the heart.

(7) The power to be quiet is
power for worship. It is essential
to prayer, and to the receiving of
the full benefit of our gathering
together from time to time for the
social rites of religion. The best
things do not force themselves
unbidden upon us; we must be
prepared to receive them, prepared
to meet our God. It would
change some of our familiar forms
of speech if we realised how
possible it is that when we are
complacently dismissing a religious service as "dull," we may
in that judgment be passing
sentence upon ourselves, and be

condemning our own unserious and unthoughtful moods and habits.

(8) The power to be quiet is the condition of all noble and fruitful activity. To be busy does not always mean to be fruitful. Many so-called busy men, both in the world and in the Church, are painfully barren and uninteresting, and their bustling activities add little to the sum of human good. Industry, enterprise, and zeal are not everything. The contemplative side of life has its pressing claims. True and sound progress in almost every sphere depends, equally alike, on action and thought. To be practical does not mean to be shallow. What we do depends ultimately upon what we are. Without the power to be quiet our work must suffer in quality, and become woefully superficial and defective.

(9) Amid the care and strife of our common life how much we need the power to be quiet! It

is pitiful to be at the mercy of things which are but the incidents of a brief and passing day. To be strong and brave we must have root in ourselves. To get out of life a Divine education we must have the quiet and well-balanced mind which in prosperity keeps us humble and in adversity patient. The power to be quiet means power to suffer and be strong, power to compel losses to yield us some moral gain, and out of temporal defeat to wrest an eternal victory.

It may seem hardly possible for us who live in these days to get and to keep the power to be quiet. Life has changed, and the whole state of society is different from what it was even fifty years ago. Simplicity is going out of fashion. We have no love for quiet things. Even home and church are suffering from the excitement and the supply of the means of excitement which are characteristic

of our time. What a constant
rush are the lives of many men
and women! Quiet work, quiet
pleasure, quiet feeling, quiet
thought, quiet prayer are things
of which they appear to be
utterly ignorant. They must
spend even their holidays in
crowds, and the noise of the big
town or city has become such a
part of their nature that they
must have the echo of it among
the hills and by the sea. They
have no power to be quiet.

> They chatter, nod, and hurry by,
> And never once possess their souls
> Before they die.

It is possible, however, to cultivate
and preserve the power to be
quiet—the quietude not of weakness but of strength, not of
passion exhausted but of passion
controlled and used, not of a world
renounced but of a world subdued
to the service of the soul and the
obedience of Christ.

Meditation will help us—frequent pauses in our busy days for serious reflection upon life's meaning and end, and for cherishing those highest thoughts which come not in noisy but in silent hours. *Prayer* will help us—the prayer that brings the sense of the Unseen Presence into our life, and the quickening and sustaining thought of the Eternal Goodness and Care ; the prayer that means the identification of the human will with the Divine will— rest in God. *The Worship of the Church* will help us—correcting and enlarging our individualism by giving us the sense of universal and eternal relationships. *Obedience* will help us. Great peace have they whose obedience to the highest and best is quick and constant ; who, instead of getting away from things, seek rather to get right with things, to be reconciled to the Divine order of the world and life, reconciled to

5

God. It is the peace of Jesus
which the world cannot give nor
take away, but which enables one
to be quiet in the world, to
venture abroad into all its excitements and strifes with a calm and
brave heart, and, while seeking
things temporal, to win with them
and through them all the finest
and most enduring things of life.

An Advent Meditation.

" He cometh with clouds."—REVELATION I. 7.

THE exhortation, " Prepare to meet thy God," which comes to us across many centuries, has in view life, and not only death; this world, and not only the next. Daily and hourly God is coming to us, and we must train ourselves to be sensitive to His presence and influence, make ourselves ready to discern and find Him. Without constant vigilance and effort we shall soon become blind and dull to the Divine aspects of the world and life.

Yes! God is constantly coming to us. He comes in the clear light of the sky, in every blue day, in the loveliness, sweetness, and bounty of the world; in all gentle affections, sweet charities, and

brave fidelities ; in every loving and
faithful heart that blesses us ; in
every fair example that wins us ; in
everything that makes life beautiful, and dear, and sacred.   Why
should we think of our God only
in connection with what is extra-
ordinary   and   terrible?   Why
should we think of great accidents
and misfortunes as if they only
were "Divine visitations"?   We
have too much of the old Paganism
still in our blood. The exceptional
is widely regarded as especially
Divine, and God is conceived as
more fully and immediately present
in His strange work of judgment
than in His unfailing daily mercies.
Let us cease to be such foolish and
unbelieving children.   Let us prepare to meet God in the beauty
and sweetness of the world, and in
all the gentle and gracious sanctities of life.   For there is nothing,
except our sin, which is not full of
God.   And everything is d ivinely
wonderful.

But in the Scriptures, old and new, we are told that God cometh with clouds, that clouds and darkness are round about Him, that He maketh the clouds His chariot, that the clouds are the dust of His feet, and that His glory is in the clouds. Clouds play a large and important part in the poetry of the Bible, as they do in the pageantry of nature. In Hebrew symbolism they represent the mystery of the Divine presence and manifestation. Yes! God cometh with clouds. Not only is He present in the bright and radiant things which surround and form part of our passing days, but in things gloomy and oppressive, which sometimes tempt us to think that for us the charm of life has vanished for ever. But the darkness as well as the light lies within the circle of the infinite harmony, and the clouds answer to and fulfil the will of God, which is a good will to all mankind.

Taken most literally, how true
the words are : "He cometh with
clouds." The clouds are such a
familiar sight that, as with most
common things, we are strangely
insensible to their beauty and
blessing. We rush here and there
over half the world in search of
sights, but we hardly lift our eyes
to gaze on the pictures of wondrous
loveliness and glory which Nature
is producing right above our heads
every day of the year. Among
natural phenomena there is hardly
anything more marvellous, more
full of divinity, than are the clouds
to him who has the eye to see, the
soul to feel, and the mind to
reflect. It is not surprising that
in every age they have been regarded as the dwelling-place of
Deity. Here the ancient exhortation is required : "Prepare to meet
thy God." We cannot receive this
heavenly manifestation unless we
are prepared for it. It is given
only to those for whom it is pre-

pared—that is, to souls prepared
for it.

Who no inward beauty has
No outward beauty sees,
Though all around be beautiful.

How little many of us discern in
nature! It is no convincing proof
of our culture that we see forms,
movements, and tints in the clouds
after they have been pointed out
to us by painter and poet. We read
Ruskin's great chapters on "The
Truth of Skies and Clouds," and we
are filled with wonder and delight;
but it required that gifted teacher
to reveal and interpret, to make us
look up and perceive a little part
of the infinite splendour that had
been a long time with us unrecog-
nised. It is good when our artists
and poets do so much for us, but
they only fulfil their ministry of
mediation when they send us back
to nature and life more able and
eager to see for ourselves the
pictures that shine and the poems

that are written there for all who
have eyes to see. We must cultivate the power that looks, not
merely at things, but into things.
To have the fine vision and insight
we must have the fine mind and
soul. Our spiritual condition is
sorrowful if the visions of gloom
and glory in the heavens above us
fail to touch our hearts, to raise
our souls, to overshadow us with
the Divine presence and make us
feel—Behold! He cometh with
clouds.

The more material uses of the
clouds are also a veritable advent
and revelation of God. The more
we think, not only of their beauty
and mystery, and the part they
play in the culture of man's higher
nature, but of the varied ways in
which they contribute to make the
earth habitable and agreeable, and
help to support and comfort the
children of men, the more we must
feel with the Hebrew poet, "Thy
faithfulness reacheth unto the

clouds," and with the seer of Patmos, "He cometh with clouds." We see God wherever we see wisdom and goodness. The presence of wisdom and goodness in material nature is the real presence of God.

But it is the symbolic meaning of the words we are considering that is their true meaning. In the history of the world, in the history of the Church and in individual experience, God has often come to men in clouds, in bewildering darkness and mystery, in great sorrows and strifes. The study of the geologic ages reveals the first advent of the Eternal Power on this earth to have been with clouds. It is a story of upheaving and convulsion, of fierce struggles and triumphs. But over all, in all, and through all we can see God. During these long, dark, chaotic ages we behold life rising slowly but steadily, and the result at last explaining and vindicating the process. And if

God was in the clouds which
preceded and accompanied the
appearance of the human race on
this planet, much more was He
and is He in the history of
man's making and training. That
history, it is true, is full of
tragedy; a darkness rests upon
our human life, which at times
appears so gross as to make
almost impossible the thought
that it could ever have been the
pavilion and scene of the creative
energy of Divine holiness and
goodness. But as we patiently
watch and study the outcome we
are moved to exclaim: Behold!
He cometh with clouds.

We look back through the centuries and observe many great
historical events which we now
clearly see to have been real
comings of God to the world; but
they came, as the Divine advents
often do come, with clouds, attended with many and vast evils—
war, bloodshed, persecution, crime,

scepticism, civil, social, religious disorganisation and wreck. At first sight they look like terrible calamities, of which we can only think with horror and lamentation. Amid the scenes of unspeakable suffering and wickedness which took place when Jerusalem went down before the power of Rome, even true believers in God might have seen or feared only evil. But the Son of Man came then in the clouds of heaven with power and great glory. That revolution established His religion on a spiritual and catholic foundation. Out of the confusion and conflict His truth and spirit came forth to men's sight in worthier and diviner form. He ceased to be a national Christ and His Church a Jewish sect, and began to be known as the Light of the world, the Saviour of mankind, the true Lord and Leader of all faithful souls.

What evils attended the event

we call the Protestant Reforma-
tion! From the point of view of
culture it appeared to the German
poet to be nothing less than a
calamity which threw back the
progress of mankind for centuries.
Unquestionably it was in certain
respects a serious loss, religiously
as well as intellectually. But
revolution was inevitable. The
changes which Luther sought had
been long and vainly sought in
more peaceful ways. They had to
wait for the violent storm which
swept away along with much
intolerable evil much real good.
But God came with the clouds.
When we muse on the great
Christian ideas which the Refor-
mation reintroduced into the
thought and life of mankind, and
the new spirit which it quickened,
we cannot but regard it as one of
the advents of the Christ of God
to our world.

We, too, are living in critical
and eventful times. Not a few

believe that the clouds and darkness which accompanied the dis-
solution of ancient civilisation will
soon cover our sky and the whole
scenery of our life. There is unrest and agitation everywhere, the
relaxing of old restraints, and
the decay of authority—of all
authority, at least, that has not its
roots struck deep down in the true
nature of things. Upon us the ends
of a world have indeed come. But
let us not be faithless. Our trusts
are truer than our fears. God is
our refuge and strength. Tumult
and confusion are His heralds.
He cometh with the clouds—in all
these complications of disintegra-
tion and change. He unmakes
only to recreate. The old earth,
full of injustice and inhumanity,
is giving place to an earth wherein
dwelleth righteousness and love.
It is but slowly the Christian ideas
and the Christian spirit win the
victory, but they are winning it.
Every great crisis in the history of

the world is a coming of the Son
of Man. It is a factor and agent
in the evolution of that Divine
Humanity of which Jesus Christ
is the Messiah.

The Day of the Lord is at hand, at
　　hand;
Its storms roll up the sky;
The nations sleep, starving on heaps of
　　gold;
All dreamers toss and sigh;
The night is darkest before the morn;
When the pain is sorest the child is
　　born,
And the Day of the Lord is at hand.

And in the Church, as in the
world, it is a time of critical strain
and trial—a day of judgment to
all our institutions, and a last day
to some of them. To the superficial
observer everything seems to be
tending towards chaos. But there
is no danger of chaos. God
cometh in the clouds, and His
Spirit is moving upon the face of
the waters. Everywhere we see
the signs of a great religious

reconstruction. The movement is
not from faith to no faith, but
from faith to more and better
faith. The sign of the Son of
Man is in the heavens. The old
prophecy, "I go away that I may
come again," is being fulfilled all
around us. Christ is coming to us
in a more glorious body, and in
Spirit more perfectly Divine,
coming in larger inspirations of
faith, and hope, and love, and
coming to-day, as yesterday, to
bring us to ourselves, to our
brethren, and to God. Even so
come, Lord Jesus!

And not only in the life of the
Church and the world, but in the
individual life it is everlastingly
true that God cometh with clouds,
with storms which darken and
trouble our mortal day, and sometimes bring the fabric of our
happiness to the ground. It is a
Pagan moralist who tells us that
we alter the nature of our misfortunes by putting a different con-

struction upon them. He did not
mock his fellows in giving them
that counsel. The construction he
meant is involved in the relations
of our darkest estate, and will
some time appear therein. When
we see what our adversities,
struggles, disappointments, and be-
reavements have done for us in
the way of deepening and refining
our nature and life; how they
have made us more thoughtful,
serious, sympathetic, and drawn
us deeper into the fellowship of
Christ, then we begin to represent
our sorrows differently, to give
them a more religious and hopeful
interpretation, to confess, Behold!
God came with the clouds, and

> To feel, although no tongue can prove,
> That every cloud that spreads above,
> And veileth love, itself is love.

O Thou who art the Soul of
goodness in things evil, teach us
how to suffer and be strong. Help
us to cherish the spirit which brings

good out of evil, and prevents adversities and disappointments from
embittering the heart and spoiling
the life.   Comfort us with a deep
sense of Thy goodness in all the
varied passages of our earthly experience, and keep us in strength
and truth, simplicity and serenity
of spirit to the end of our days.
Amen.

The Christian Conception of the World and Life.

"The world . . . life . . . things present . . . all are yours, and ye are Christ's, and Christ is God's."—1 COR. III. 22, 23.

THE divineness or sacredness of the present world and the present life is one of the great lessons which in our day we have had set to learn. It is a Christian idea, but its development, like that of all large and living ideas, has been painfully slow and complicated. For many hundreds of years it has been sedulously taught in the name of Christ, and it has been more or less the belief of men, that the kingdom of God is not now and here, but in the future, and in another place. It is not difficult to explain, and in a measure to justify, the attitude of primitive, mediæval, and Puritan Christianity

toward the world and life. Yet
there can be little doubt that the
separatist attitude is not the true
Christian attitude. The incarnation—that perfect union of the
Divine and human in the person
of Jesus Christ, of which the con-
stitution of man has always been a
prophecy—is the consecration of
our nature and life. Through
Him whose birth we celebrate
every returning Christmas we
know the world of natural rela-
tionship to be a Divine world;
fatherhood and motherhood, child-
hood and brotherhood, our human
love and friendship, have had their
ideal significance and beauty un-
veiled, and the families of the earth
have been blessed.

The feeling of Jesus toward the
world was not that of the ascetic
or pessimist. He was in love with
this earth and this earthly life.
He had all a poet's delight in sky
and landscape, in every touch of
natural beauty, and not less

delight but more in the world of
men and women. He liked to feel
the warmth and magnetism of
human neighbourhood, and was at
home among crowds. Most truly
and deeply He entered into our
human life. The variety and
breadth of His sympathies were a
surprise and revelation to many in
Galilee and Judea. So little of an
ascetic was He that by one class
of religionists He was set down as
entirely too loose in his ideas of
meat and drink and social intercourse. His goodness was genial
and loveable, and had all that
charm which touches and wins the
heart. His communion with God
did not mean separation from men.
In the spirit and practice of His
life earth and heaven, life here
and life hereafter, were not op-
posed to each other. In this
world He did not feel that He was
absent from God. He had en-
veloping His whole life, and
vitalising every part of it, the

sense of His Father's presence and
companionship. He not only came
forth from His Father and was
going back to His Father, but He
saw His Father everywhere, and
was nowhere alone, because His
Father was with Him. He sought
all through His ministry to inspire
His disciples and friends with the
confidence which was the spiritual
atmosphere of His own life, that
even here on earth and in this
present life they were children in
their Father's house.

It is wonderful how very little
Jesus said about the mere con-
tinuance of life—life hereafter.
We can only be sure of some five
or six great sayings which have a
plain and direct reference to
another world. The parables and
prophecies which later Christianity
transferred to life after death, a
more careful examination has
shown, were originally connected
with a different order of ideas.
The kingdom of God on earth is

the central principle of Christ's teaching. Around it is grouped all that He said and taught. "As in heaven so on earth," is the Lord's ideal and prayer.

To win and keep the Christian faith in immortality we must recognise the essential unity of the two lives and the two worlds. It is one life we live on earth and in heaven. Heaven is for those who have made the most and the best of earth. Until we have got the Divine good out of this world we have rightfully but small concern with any other world. The Gospel assumes that a man cannot believe in the next life till he believes in this life. The sense of a larger life beyond will not make itself clear and commanding till the Divine significance of this life has been learned. It is life that is the assurance and revelation of life. To raise the quality of life before death, to make life fuller and deeper, was therefore the

object of the Saviour's mission.
"I am come that they might have
life, and that they might have
it more abundantly." Immortality
is revealed to man by revealing it
in man. When life takes on the
Christ-like quality it becomes itself
the prophecy of more life; we have
no doubt or fear about the future;
there comes surely if gradually a
great trust and hope, a great peace,
a sense of encompassment by
eternal goodness, a joy unspeakable and full of glory.

The attitude of Jesus Christ
towards the world and life must be
our attitude, His faith our faith,
His spirit our spirit. To be a
Christian is to be a man after the
order and type of Jesus Christ; it
is to think as He thought, feel as
He felt, live as He lived; it is to
take and keep His attitude toward
God and man, toward heaven and
earth, toward life here and life
hereafter. Taking His mind and
spirit as our law and guide we

know that this world is God's as
well as the next, and that God is
here as well as there. We are not
journeying toward a remote Deity,
but walking with God. He only
finds God who finds Him now and
here. God wants us to love and
enjoy His world. We can " serve
Him with mirth." "All things
are yours, things present as well
as things to come, because ye are
Christ's and Christ is God's."
Why should we be afraid to set
our lives in harmony with this
truth ? We are not servants, but
children in the house of God. We
need not take our pleasures by
stealth. " Touch not, taste not,
handle not," is a maxim only
quoted by the Christian Apostle to
be condemned. It is not by nega-
tions and prohibitions we can save
ourselves or others. To be kept
out of the way of temptation and
danger is plainly not the Divine
way of saving and training men.
The guarded life is not the safest

life. Wise restraint is necessary
until character is well formed and
disciplined, but it is character that
is the real and ultimate protection.
Commerce and culture need not be
anti-Christian. The Christian faith
and spirit are meant to influence
the world as a renewing principle
taking full possession of the natural
life, rather than as a destructive
principle crushing it. All things
may serve the soul. "All things
are yours" to use, not abuse. The
limitation of liberty may be a
temporary necessity, but to learn
how to use everything aright is
the fundamental law and lesson.
Natural joys may blend with Divine
sanctities. In and through the
earthly things we may find the
heavenly realities. We may eat
and drink to the glory of God.
Sacred and pathetic memories,
spiritual ideas and affections, were
associated by our Lord with a
supper. "Christianity," says
Novalis in a suggestive sentence,

"is the capability of everything earthly to become the bread and wine of a Divine life." Deep in the fellowship of Jesus Christ we learn to take a gracious and bright view of life—even of its hardest conditions and limitations. We learn that there is good in everything save sin, that sin is the only real evil of life, that these mortal years and all their circumstances and experiences mean education— the Father educating His children.

In many ways and by many agencies God is teaching us this great Christian lesson, that here and now we are children in our Father's house and fulfilling in present human experience the prophetic words: "Now, therefore, ye are no more strangers and pilgrims, but members of the household of God." Every energy of our civilisation is reducing the ancient ills of life, making the world look less and less inhospitable and harsh, and more and

more homelike.   By the removal
of hardships, by the growth of
justice, and that disposition which
is fitly named "the enthusiasm of
humanity," by the spread of
education, and the multiplication
of pure and noble interests and
pleasures, we are being slowly
brought to a new and more
Christian sense of the value and
sacredness of the present world
and the present life.

It has been a common test of
the reality and depth of a man's
religious life to be able to say,
"I am willing and ready to die,"
but a truer and healthier conception has entered into the
thoughts of men.   It is good to
live.   In this world and to-day it
is good to live.   To make this life
as great and sacred as it ever can
be; to taste as many sweet and
solemn joys as we are able; to
throw ourselves, mind, heart, and
soul into the work of helping the
world, and enabling the lives we

touch on every side to find and experience the goodness of existence; to bear quietly and bravely the hard and sorrowful realities of our personal lot as the beneficent discipline of Heaven—this is being more and more clearly seen by us to be the purpose of pure Christianity; and striving to be obedient to this Heavenly vision, we feel that we are making for whatever awaits us beyond—the truest and amplest preparation.

The Immanent God.

" Quench not the Spirit."—1 Thess. v. 19.

THERE are some truths which we learn slowly and somewhat reluctantly. How slow we are to recognise and appreciate the significance of that lofty spiritual conception of God as the ever-present indwelling Life of the world, which in these days is making all things new! We think of God as far off, and as only present with the world, now and again, at certain points of time and in certain places. We find it difficult to believe and realise that He is ever near; not only beyond the world but in the world; not only the Ruler of man from without, but the pervading and quickening Spirit of his secret life.

It is not a mere dream of the
poetic and devout mind that God
is present everywhere in His
universe, but a truth of reason
and faith. The Divine immanence
is the highest conception we can
reach of the Divine relation to the
world and life. Creation is in-
stinct with the Spirit of God. In
its law and forces reside Divine
Intelligence and Will. The things
we see around us have no life of
their own; in God they live and
move. The loveliness of the world
is the light of His countenance.
He is the Power, the Wisdom, the
Beauty, the Severity, the Gentle-
ness, the Goodness we behold in
nature.

But the Eternal Spirit who fills
heaven and earth with His glory
is present in a fuller and higher
measure in man. It is not our
nature that separates us from
God, but evil conduct and character. God, and Christ, and man
are of one nature. We are God's

kindred, says St. Paul. He is the Father of our spirits. His essential nature is our essential nature; His essential life is our essential life. There is something of God in every man—a germ of Divine life. There is no such creature as "a mere man"—a man in whom there is no breath or spark of Godhead. The idea of the Incarnation is profoundly true; we only require to enlarge it. God in Christ remains, and must remain, the central fact and truth of the Christian religion; but it is also true that Christ is the revelation and prophecy of the Divine Presence and Life in humanity. It is the end for which God reveals Himself that the Divine may live in the human, that God may dwell in man, and man dwell in God. Not God in sacramental bread and wine, but God in man is the Real Presence.

Nothing can be simpler than the doctrine or teaching concerning

the Holy Spirit as we find it in the
Bible, before it has been hardened
into a dogma, and beset and
embarrassed by speculative questions and disputes. It is just this:
God not only dwells in the material
universe, and not only in Jesus
Christ, but in all men in more or
less degree, the Life of their life,
the source and inspiration of all
that is fair and worthy. The gift
of the Spirit is not something for
which we have to wait; we have it
now in our nature and life, and we
shall have it more and more
according to our faithfulness to
what we have already received.
Everything in us that is good and
not evil; all noble faculty and
affection; all truth, wisdom, purity
and love; all the hidden influences
which move our minds and hearts
to better things; all those sugges-
tions and impulses which have
sometimes been foolishly described
as " mere natural goodness "—all
are the movements and signs of

the indwelling and inspiring Spirit
of God.

In the sacred Scriptures we are
bidden reverence ourselves, and
reverence all men. And to do this
we have only to know ourselves as
we truly are. Let us believe in
the indwelling God. Let us
believe in that Divine inspiration
which is the soul's native endow-
ment, also in that Divine inspiration which is continually proffered,
and by which our life may be
quickened and unfolded immeasur-
ably. Every impulse or yearning
after good is the presence and
pressure of the Divine Spirit in
the human spirit. We quench the
Spirit of God when, by our care-
lessness or neglect of self-discipline,
we allow anything that is good in
us to fade away and perish—any
natural faculty or aptitude, any
true affection, any fine feeling,
any right moral or religious impulse, any spiritual aspiration.

(1) In the Bible such endow-

ments as physical strength,
mechanical skill, mental acuteness,
and wisdom are spoken of as
the presence and inspiration of the
Spirit of God in man. We do not,
as a rule, think of the Divine Spirit
as inspiring men to design build-
ings and furniture, to work in gold
and silver and brass, to discover
the secrets of nature, and to ad-
minister national affairs. We con-
fine the Most High to clerical, mis-
sionary and evangelistic matters.
Our life is practically atheistic,
"without God," except so far as
the interests of the individual soul
and of the Church are concerned.
But the Bible is right, and our
ordinary thought about ordinary
life is wrong. We have nothing
which we have not received. Every
good gift cometh down from God.
It is the inspiration of the present
God which still enables men to do
all manner of skilful work, to
invent, and plan, and execute, to
make discoveries, and to think

rightly. Must not this be the true and supreme end of all education and discipline—so to quicken, develop and strengthen the natural faculties that they may be the fit instruments or channels through which the Divine Spirit may communicate His thought and reveal His will—His thought and will, not only concerning ecclesiastical and purely religious concerns, but concerning all the manifold interests of the wide human world in which we live?

We resist the Spirit when we do not make the most and the best of our natural endowments or gifts; and we quench the Spirit when, through the neglect of proper training and exercise, we allow any such gifts to grow less, and finally, to die out, as any gift will that is not wisely and constantly cultivated. Men quench the Spirit by allowing the sensual nature to act as a drag upon their energy. We have heard a master say of a

workman : " He is not the man he
was, he has not the same power
and skill since he took to drink."
We have heard much the same
thing said of lawyers and doctors,
artists and preachers. We have
seen with our own eyes indolence,
intemperance, sensuality, the lust of
money and social position, pride,
envy and malice injuring the finer
capabilities of men, killing their
intellectual force, and sometimes
destroying that mysterious power
or gift to which we give the name
of genius. Now what does all this
mean when we look at things in
the light of God? It means that
this man and that man have been
quenching the Spirit—the power
God gave them in order to be
something and to do something,
to serve their generation, and to
be helpful to the world. Let us
not by laziness, neglect, or disobedience quench the Spirit—dissipate or destroy the gifts which
are the inspiration of the Almighty.

(2) The spirit of truth in man
is the presence and activity in our
thought and feeling of the God of
truth. To resist the impulse that
urges us to seek after truth is to
resist the movement of the Divine
mind in our minds, and to stifle
conviction is to quench the Spirit.
How effectually do worldliness and
bigotry quench the Spirit of truth!
All that many people want in life
is money, or social position, or a
comfortable and easy time of it;
and possessed and ruled by such
vulgar aims they have little care
for truth. But selfishness is not
always coarse; it is sometimes
very refined, taking on plausible
and subtle forms and calling itself
love of family and love of church.
Too many men and women are
lovers of themselves rather than
lovers of truth. Let no selfish
passion, no worldly aim, no sec-
tarian ambition, no fear, no
vanity, no prejudice, no love of
quietness, no love of party or

church, ever tempt us to resist
the Spirit of truth.   Let us
reverence and be loyal to conviction.   It is the love of truth
that brings salvation to the mind.
Indifference to truth is atheism to
God.   God is the deepest self of
every man.   A man untrue to
what is best in himself—to honest
and serious conviction—is untrue
to God.

(3) The sense of right in man is
the presence and movement of the
Spirit, which he is exhorted not to
quench.   What is called conscience
—that voice rising from the depths
of our being which speaks to us of
duty, and troubles, if it does not
destroy the comfort of every ex-
cuse we can make for disobedience,
is in truth what our fathers said
it was—the voice of God, though
sometimes   misinterpreted;   the
utterance of an   obligation   we
apprehend, but   do   not   create.
We resist and are in danger of
quenching the Spirit of God when

we refuse to be led by our feeling
of right, by our sense of duty;
when we are disobedient to the
whispers of conscience, to our
inward drawings toward good
and our inward shrinkings from
evil. The sense of right is the
disclosure of obligation and the
call to obedience. Conscience is
not infallible, yet there is no surer
way of getting to the real truth
and right of things than by
obedience to the highest and best
we know. Unto the upright there
ariseth light in the darkness. By
obedience, by throwing ourselves
into union with our feelings of
right and making haste to obey
them, we are certain to win the
guidance we seek and need. But
if we trifle with conscientious
impulse and scruple, and try to
argue right that which is plainly
wrong, we are in danger of com-
mitting the awful sin of quenching
the Spirit of God: in danger of
destroying the moral sense and of

turning the light that is in us to darkness.

(4) The feelings which stand apart from our selfish cravings, and which urge us to help others; the impulses of love, pity, generosity, and sympathy—what are they but the presence and movement of the Divine Spirit in the human heart? Let us identify ourselves, not with our lower but with our higher nature; not with our selfish, but with our unselfish affections and impulses. Love is of God, for God is love. "He that dwelleth in love dwelleth in God, and God in him." Let us beware of harbouring the anti-social feelings and passions, such as malice, envy, unforgiveness and the disposition to put the claims of private wellbeing before everything else. Let us ever remember that we are free to cherish or to quench our highest impulses. The Divine action in and on man is not mechanical, but moral; it is

not coercion, but impulse and
suggestion; not compulsory force,
but quickening influence.   We
can resist the Spirit of God—
resist wilfully and violently and
resist by our undesigned neglect
and indifference.

(5) We have moments and experiences in life when we feel God
to be more than near, when we
become acquainted with the ca-
pacities and possibilities of our
nature and life, and we apprehend
what is meant by the essential
unity of God and man, and realise
the communion of the Holy Spirit.
Trifle, forget and disobey as we
may, yet we have our serious
hours.   We are not the petty,
superficial creatures we sometimes
take ourselves and our fellows to
be.   Not only around us but
within us there is the mystery of
God.   Our nature is deeper than
we know or are capable of knowing.   Our littleness and shallow-
ness are only seeming.   Mind,

heart and soul draw their life from
infinite sources. We are related
to all that is most Divine in the
universe. And we have experiences which make us aware of all
this; experiences awful yet glorious with indwelling God, and
which bring with them new and
wonderful accessions of spiritual
light and impulse. The worldly
mind, considered in itself, may be
enmity against God; but men of
the world are not wholly worldly.
They have their deeper and better
moments—moments of inspiration,
of self-surprise and self-revelation.

No man can think, nor in himself per-
    ceive,
Sometimes at waking, in the street
    sometimes,
Or, on the hillside, always unforewarned
A grace of finer being, a larger life upon
His own impinging, to which his own
    seems
But thick cloud to make that visible,
Touched by a sudden glory round the
    edge.

Such inspirations we all have,

hours of moral exaltation when
the Spirit of God breathes upon
our life and kindles to a warm
glow the fires of spiritual affection
and impulse. Let us obey these
heavenly visions. Let us have the
courage to live by the truest and
highest revealed to us. The life
of our best hours and experiences
is our true life. Not to strive to
make these best hours the standard
by which we daily live, to be
disloyal to that which we see and
worship and love in the most
exalted and radiant moments of
our existence, to make no effort to
preserve and perpetuate the glory
of this occasional spiritual life, is
to resist and quench the Spirit.

O God, the Holy Spirit of our
secret life, the Unseen Source and
Root of all our goodness,—of all
the good thoughts we have ever
thought, of all the good feelings
we have ever cherished, and of all
the good deeds we have ever done;
give us grace, we pray Thee, to

covet earnestly the best gifts, to nourish and maintain the things that are simple and true, and always to offer unto Thee the sacrifice of a consecrated and faithful life. Amen.

The Value of a Day.

" Are there not twelve hours in the day?"
JOHN II. 9.

THE one art, it has been said, which man has never learned is to take the things that are now and here at their real worth. Even our religion, in its common interpretations, spends too much time on the things that have been or are to come. The past and the future absorb by far the larger part of the interest of too many. We need to recall our minds from yesterday and to-morrow, to consider the worth of the present and and passing day.

1. *To-day—How Related to Yesterday and To-morrow.*

The secret of true living is to be found in making the most of each day. We are putting yesterday to its truest and noblest use when we are using its experience to make the life of to-day better. We are preparing for the morrow in the truest and noblest way when we are striving with all our might to be faithful to the opportunity of to-day. To spend to-day in looking away from it, backward to yesterday, or forward to the morrow, is simply fatal to the highest purposes and issues of life.

It is true that the power of looking before and after is one of the most characteristic endowments of man. And it is not denied that there is a way of living in the present which makes impossible all best efforts and attainments. We are certainly not making the most of to-day if we are not bringing to bear upon its events, relations, and duties the wisdom drawn from the experience of yesterday, and the

inspiration that comes from the
thought of the morrow.

Memory has its gracious and
serious uses.   It may be good,
now and again, to yield ourselves to
the spell of past things. To be taken
away for a brief moment from our
exciting and exacting life into the
peace of yesterday may refresh
and strengthen us, rescue us from
depressed feelings and narrow
views, enable us to perceive and
appreciate better the opportunity
of the present, and renew our
energy for the never - ending
struggle. We are making a good
use of the yesterdays of our life
when we are taking their lessons
to heart, in order to protect and
improve the life of the new day
that is passing over us.

And, if we are truly wise, we shall
not be indifferent to the past of the
life of mankind and its teaching.
It will at least show us that certain
ways of dealing with our great
speculative and practical questions

lead to certain conclusions and results, and thus save us from a very tragic waste of time and energy. Universal history has been called "a kind of memory" for the race; it is also a kind of Bible—part of that larger and equally Divine Bible whose canon is never closed. Sound progress is ever conservative of all that is finest and best in the old life it leaves behind; it does not allow one jot of true substance, one tittle of true worth, to pass away till it is fulfilled in something truer and better.

And "looking before" may sometimes be as much a duty as "looking after." Experience teaches us the need of the onlooking and expectant spirit. We are saved by hope from discouragement and despair, saved also from indolence and ignoble contentment with ourselves and our surroundings. In our hopefulness lies the spring of progress and the promise

of achievement. The hopeful
temper, kindled and fed by faith
in the Eternal Goodness, is the
temper of inspiration. It is the
temper of all the great teachers
and leaders of the race. And the
humblest man, moving among
simplest duties, requires some
touch of it to redeem his life from
pettiness and vulgarity. It is
essential to the working out of
that great salvation, whose watch-
words are Character and Service,
that one should feel that his life
is linked to Divine purposes and
movements. " Where there is no
vision the people perish." To-
morrow gives larger and deeper
significance to the life of to-day.

Granting then, as we may do
most readily, that a true and noble
life is only possible by bringing
to bear upon to-day the experience
of yesterday and the hope of to-
morrow, yet this concession does
not diminish the value of to-day.
We are not to live as if to-day

stood alone—unrelated and apart;
but we are called to live in to-day
—in to-day, not in yesterday;
in to-day, not in to-morrow. We
have to guard against that kind of
looking back, and that kind of
looking forward, which would
tempt us to forget or slight the
claims and duties, on the fulfilment of which depend the pre-
servation of the best life of the
past, and the realisation of the
best hopes we can cherish for the
future. We have to fight against
moods and habits of thought and
feeling which breed indifference
to the present and contempt for
it.   The past and the future,
yesterday and to-morrow, are not
being wisely used when they are
robbing to-day of interest and
meaning; when we are so absorbed by memories or expectations that we have not energy
enough to make the most and best
of the present opportunity.

Let us be loyal to the life of to-day. Let us not give to yesterday more than its due. True life means unresting movement, aspiration, and endeavour. Even the man of many years is but beginning life, and cannot spare much time for recollection and regret. What we experienced or achieved yesterday is but small when compared with what remains. Let us, on the other hand, while cherishing the hope and prophecy of to-morrow, not sink into mere dreamers. The glory we see and seek cannot be born without our whole-hearted co-operation. Let us make of our heavenly visions inspirations to present activity. The man of faith ought to be the man of works, and the most ideal man the most practical man.

II. *To-day—its importance.*

To-day is the supreme and critical moment of life. Our vital concern is ever with to-day. Life in to-day is a clear and impressive feature of Biblical teaching. The Bible delights in the present tense. " Now " is its accepted and saving time. The emphasis of both Testaments is on to-day. " To-day if ye will hear His voice harden not your hearts." " I must work while it is day." To look back is, in the judgment of the Master of our life, to unfit ourselves for any share in the work of the kingdom of God. To be loyal to the Christian idea and order of life, we must be ready to break with the old for the sake of the new. With absolute rigour Jesus Christ ever insisted upon this heroic renunciation of the past, and this heroic obedience to the present inspiration. " Let the dead bury their dead, follow thou Me." " He that saveth his life shall lose it."

" Be not anxious for the morrow " is another great Gospel saying. It was spoken to raise the troubled heart above all undue

and useless care, and with a view
to the concentration of thought
and energy on the duty of to-day.
It is a word perfectly true and
wise. It is folly to try to grasp
too much of life at once. To take
the days one by one is Divine
wisdom. A day may seem but a
small section of time to measure
and command, but it holds about
as much care and responsibility as
our minds can embrace and bear.
The only way to save ourselves
from a past, the memory of which
will be a reproach and a burden, is
to care well for each new day
before it leaves us to take its place
among the irrevocable yesterdays.
The only way to prepare for the
morrow is through fidelity to the
duty of to-day. To-day found us
as yesterday left us; to-morrow
will find us as to-day leaves us.

There is little need, then, to
dwell on the past. It is not behind us. In a very real sense it
goes with us. Names pass away,

but forces abide. We stand to-
day in vital moral connection with
all the days we have ever lived.
The yesterdays are still with us to
bless, or to curse. It is true, in a
way, that each new day may be a
new beginning, and that there is
never a point in life when we may
not move on to something better,
and yet each new day is the outcome of the day before. The new
continues, it does not efface the
old. There is no "dead past;"
the past is living in the present.
We cannot get away from these
inexorable yesterdays. Their life
lives in what we are to-day; in the
fibre and quality of mind and soul;
in thought and feeling; in taste,
tendency, and habit; in everything that goes to make up what
we call character. "God requireth
that which is past." The good
and the ill we do find us out.
We reap what we sow. Every
act of every day has its effect
upon our character. Our present

character is the Divine judgment upon our past conduct. The "Great White Throne" is not far away in the future. Here and now it is set up in its majesty. Every day we stand at the bar of God. Every day is a doomsday. The Divine justice does not require the machinery of a vast public trial to make manifest good and evil, to reward right-doing and punish wrong-doing. Time is part of eternity, and every day of time has in it the essence of eternity. The future will only reveal what God has been always doing.

But to-day is not only a history of the past, it is also a prophecy of the future. It is by watching to-day we can tell what will be on the morrow. Foresight is truly insight. The power to foresee and forecast is the power to discern the natural and necessary tendency and result of certain principles and habits of life. Life has no sharp epochs. There is no violent break between yesterday and to-day. Whatever is to come out of to-day exists in to-day. The future is not a revolution, but an evolution. To-day is the child and heir of yesterday; to-morrow will be the child and heir of to-day.

It is by a great perversion that so much of our religious teaching directs our thoughts to the life of to-morrow—to what follows death. It is plainly not the will of God that we should think much of the hereafter while we are here. There are seasons and pauses in life when "other worldliness" becomes the most natural and proper mood and habit of the mind, yet frequent and morbid thought about the future is a hindrance and not a help to sound Christian progress. What we are now in life and character, in our relations to God and man, is the main thing. The future can hold no promise of good, save what is laid up by present faithfulness.

In quietness and confidence we
may leave what is to happen after
death to the Everlasting Father
and Redeemer of souls, while we
assure ourselves that the only possible preparation for the worthy
use of another life is the worthy
use of this life. Strictly speaking,
there can be no special preparation for the future. The whole of
life, and not isolated acts, experiences, and hours, is the real
preparation. It is by living we
prepare to live. He who lives
faithfully and well to-day, filling
each day with truth and righteousness, love and peace, with honest
and earnest labour for God and
mankind, has no need or cause to
be anxious for the morrow. Whatever happens, it must ever in this
world, and in all the worlds, be
well with him.

3. *To-day—its Blessing and Opportunity.*

What a great and royal gift is

a day! It comes to us laden with blessing and promise, full of history and prophecy. It has taken many thousands of years to prepare it for us. In the very fuel that feeds its fires is the vegetation of primeval ages. The effort to realise the tremendous cost at which we have everything in the daily order and blessing of life is baffling even to the imagination. Every day that dawns has countless and complex relations with things far and wide.

> This to-day
> Washed Adam's feet, and streams away
> Far into yon eternity.

Ancient Egypt and Israel, Greece and Rome, Scandinavia and primitive Germany, priests and philosophers, prophets and poets, discoverers and inventors, innumerable thinkers and workers, heroes and saints, known and unknown, have helped to prepare the materials out of which to-day's

opportunity has been made. We
are the heirs of the ages in a most
real sense.   We inherit the good,
material and moral, wrought out
through the experiences of many
men and many races of men
through many centuries.   In the
life of to-day are the results of
the labour and struggle of all the
yesterdays.

Whatever of true life there was of yore
   Along our veins is springing;
For us its martyrs die, its prophets soar,
   Its poets still are singing.

"Write it on your heart," says
Emerson, "that every day is the
best day of the year." No day is
poor and commonplace—if we do
not make it so. The judgment of
the pessimist is virtually a condem-
nation of himself and his own way
of living.   To the prepared soul
every day is full of marvel and
joy. No glory has passed from
the earth. The old world is ever
a new world. Life has lost none

of its ancient fascination; it is as
full as ever of grandeur and loveliness, of wonder and mystery.
All the things which deep-seeing
men have seen to be in human
life, the things which have in-
spired the finest poetry of the
world, are in human life to-day.
Every day has its comedies and
tragedies. Genius does not invent, it discovers and interprets.
To find examples of heroism we
need not turn to classic pages, nor
search the annals of martyrdom.
Heroism is as unfailing a reality
as the daily dawn. Around and
in each day are all the great
marvels of creation, all the moral
forces and splendours of life, and
all the sacred realities to which
the deeply-moved soul has wit-
nessed in every age. The miracle
of creation is renewed every day.
Light and heat, and all the
ancient creative forces, are still
active, doing the same kind of
work they did when "the morning

stars sang together, and the first-
born of the sons of God shouted
for joy." "My Father," said
Jesus, " works continuously, and I
work." The Holy Spirit is not a
vanished influence. Revelation is
not reminiscence or report merely.
The great story of God with man,
of which the Bible is the record,
is not an exceptional episode in
the history of our race. God is
the living God and the God of the
living. What He was to prophets
and apostles He will be to us.
The difference between ages and
men in their realisation of God
is fundamentally a difference in
spiritual life and culture. God is
no respecter of ages or persons.

This time is equal to all time that's
   past ;
      .   .   .   Man is to God
What he hath ever been.

The Divine vision can be won,
and the Divine voice heard, to-day.
Personal and immediate com-

munion with God is not the
accident but the essence of religion.
In the soul is the Real Presence.
The Father is everywhere near to
His children. Every mountain may
be a point of contact between God
and man, and the foot of Jacob's
ladder may be touched anywhere.
We have in to-day all that men
ever had—the same spiritual re-
sources, the same Divine helps.
The heavenly realities belong to
the present as much as to the past
or the future. Loyalty to the
laws of the highest growth will
make to-day as sacred as yesterday,
and one of the days of heaven upon
earth. The eternal life of the
Christian Gospel stands not in
quantity but in quality of years,
and is shared by us here according
to our faithfulness.

It is a common saying that life
is but a day. It is used to express
the awful and pathetic brevity of
our life here on this earth. It is
the utterance of an impressive

truth, common yet never commonplace. But when we say each day
is a life, we are giving expression
to a truth of deeper importance,
and of greater practical value and
use. There is nothing small. In
the smallest things are the elements
of the greatest. One day of life
has in it the quality of the whole.
It is grander than we know or can
imagine. It has infinite relations.
In its acts and relations we see
God making history, and man
making his own future—making
the character which creates condition and decides destiny.

Are we making the most and
the best of the opportunities of to-
day? Many people are sighing
and crying for the larger opportunities to which they expect death
will introduce them, who do not
know the value of a day. One of
our poets has represented the days
coming to us with their faces
veiled, but when they have passed
beyond our reach and call the

draped figures become radiant, and the gifts we slighted are seen to be right royal treasures.

Daughters of Time, the hypocritic Days,
Muffled and dumb like barefoot der-
    vishes,
And marching single in an endless file,
Bring diadems and fagots in their hands.
To each they offer gifts after his will,—
Bread, kingdoms, stars, and sky that
    holds them all.
I, in my pleachéd garden, watched the
    pomp,
Forgot my morning wishes, hastily
Took a few herbs and apples, and the
    Day
Turned and departed. I, too late,
Under her solemn fillet saw the scorn.

Let us make the most and the best of each day's opportunity for pure and noble enjoyment. Let not our sorrow for some vanished good, nor our expectation of some promise or expected good, make us insensible to, or ungrateful for, the good which is now and here. Let us train our faculties to observe and appreciate all the gracious blessings of daily life. We need not be suspicious of what gives pleasure and joy. The lesson of joy is as Divine a lesson to learn as that of obedience and sacrifice.

Let us make the most and the best of each day's opportunity for thought and meditation. It was a good rule of a great man never to allow one day to pass without reading something that would quicken and enrich his mind.. The inner life constantly needs deepening. Knowledge is growing from more to more, and God is ever revealing Himself. Every day is a day of revelation. We must follow the Spirit of truth. Our highest attainments ought only to be new starting-points. The mind closed against new visions and interpretations of truth is already dying.

Let us make the most and the best of the opportunity for moral and spiritual growth and beneficent service which is afforded by the daily task. It is in the sphere

of the every-day duties most men
must win the discipline which our
earthly life is meant to yield, must
form the character which is the
crown of life, and prepare themselves for wider usefulness. No
violent, overstrained efforts are
necessary to achieve that moral
and spiritual success which Scripture calls salvation — deliverance
from weakness and sin, the recon-
ciliation of the life to the order
and will of God, the perfection of
character. We may through the
humblest fidelities reach the Christian righteousness, and rise out of
our selfishness into the Christian
generosities and sympathies. It is
only by living up to the ideal and
duty of making each day perfect
in itself that we can make life a
spiritual triumph.

There are only "twelve hours in
a day," and yet how much can be
done in and with a day.

One day with life and heart
Is more than enough to find a world.

"A day is extremely long," says
Goethe, "if only one knows how
to appreciate and employ it." The
power of working miracles has
been defined as essentially the
power to take things which every-
body has, and to do with them
what nobody else can do. The
miracle of the sun standing still is
wrought every day by earnest and
resolute men. Purpose, persever-
ance, self-control and self-devotion
can in effect arrest the flight of
time, and make the shadow go
back on the dial. The length of a
day is not to be measured by its
hours and minutes, but by what
we put into it and take out of it;
by what we think and feel, do and
strive to do, in it. It is the full
and fruitful day that is the long
day. We all have days that are
better than a thousand—golden
days that redeem months and years
of languid days. They are not
meant to be splendid isolations.
To their level of power, of service,

of joy, God would have us raise the life of every day. "The greatest value of any day," says John Foster, "ought to be taken as the fixed value of every day."

What are we doing with our days? We ought to be striving with all our might to get as much real good as we can out of them, and to do as much real good as we can in them. We cannot afford to trifle with them. No miracle will bring back the days we throw away. The opportunities of life do not repeat themselves. There is no to-morrow for the work that ought to be done to-day. The cry "Too late" is not false. The mercy of God is infinite every way, but an opportunity lost is lost for ever. Other doors may open, but that door is shut.

The exhortation, "Prepare to meet thy God," is, indeed, an exhortation to prepare for life, not death. Every day we meet God; every day we need to be prepared

to meet Him. We prepare for
what we suppose to be great days.
But every day that dawns may be
a great day, a Divine day. For
every day brings opportunities of
knowing truth, of enjoying beauty,
of doing right, of helping man,
and of serving God. Let us not
cheat ourselves of the heavenly
good. Let us be ready for every
day, that we may derive from it
its blessings. The supreme opportunities of life are not in the circumstances and seasons when we
are most clearly conscious of them.
"In such an hour as ye think not,
the Son of Man cometh." It was
on a common day the Saviour of
men met Zaccheus on the Jericho
road, and said to him, "Come
down; this day I must abide at
thy house." It was on a common
day He met the woman of Samaria
at the well, and by His conversa-
tion made that day a day of
revelation for all the ages. To-
day all good and great things are

possible.   Let us by our faith and
faithfulness, by our obedience to
all best visions and impulses, turn
it into a day of salvation, a day of
God, one of the days of the Son of
Man, one of the days of heaven
upon earth.

Forenoon, and afternoon, and night!
  Forenoon,
And afternoon, and night! Forenoon,
  and—what!
The empty song repeats itself.   No
  more ?
Yea, that is life: make this forenoon
  sublime,
This afternoon a psalm, this night a
  prayer.
And Time is conquered, and thy crown
  is won.

A Simple Gospel.

"Trust in the Lord and do good."
PSALM xxxvii. 3.

IT is good, in these days of religious questioning and strife, to get back to such a simple confession of faith as this: "Trust in the Lord and do good." This little, familiar text covers everything essential; it expresses the sum and substance of religion, and the great secret of right living. To bring us to the temper and state of trust and obedience is the end of everything; the end of our mortal discipline and experience; the end of all human aspirings and strivings, and of all Divine inspirings and revealings; the end of the ministry of Jesus Christ, and of all ministries of the Spirit and ministries of the Church.

The Son of Man lived and taught,
suffered and died, to make this
trust and obedience possible and
more possible : to bring men out
of bondage to invisible terrors and
selfish passions; to quicken and
nourish in men confidence toward
God and loyalty to the Divine
order and law of human life.

The great problem which is set
before every man is not to solve
and interpret the riddle of the
universe, but to live faithfully and
bravely his own life. We need
just so much religious assurance
and inspiration as will enable us
to do this; enough to give us
confidence, courage, hope in the
struggle of our days to be the men
and women we are meant to be
and ought to be.

There are questions concerning
life and God which we cannot
answer, mysteries which the
keenest thought cannot penetrate,
and which rise before us in every
direction in all their ancient

solemnity. And yet that matters
not, if only we can know enough
to enable us to have confidence in
the essential goodness of the universe and life; enough to nourish
the calm and deepening sense that
all is well; enough for the per-
ception and performance of duty;
enough for the culture of character; enough for the exercise of
patience, charity, and hope;
enough to inspire strength and
peace. It is just this measure of
knowledge, and no more, which
we need for the practical purposes
of life.

We do not need the knowledge
of a god to live the life and do the
work of a man; but, on the other
hand, there must be some knowledge before there can be trust,
some foundation in knowledge for
the faith which goes beyond knowledge. The God with whom we
have to do is not an austere
taskmaster, seeking to reap where
He has not sown; He gives us

grounds and reasons for trust
before He solicits trust.   In the
world of nature and man, in the
best thoughts of our own minds,
in the best affections of our own
hearts, in the best experiences of
our own lives, in the witness of
saintly and prophetic souls, in the
life and work of Jesus Christ—
God has revealed enough of His
character and will to quicken and
sustain trust in His righteousness
and love, when clouds and darkness are around about Him, and
mystery besets us behind and
before, and we cannot walk any
more by sight.

In all the range of ancient
literature we do not find anywhere
a deeper sense of the mystery of
life than in the Old Testament,
yet it is pervaded with a pure and
lofty trust in all-wise and almighty
Goodness.   From end to end it
inculcates and justifies constant
and complete confidence in God as
true wisdom.   It is full of hints

and glimpses of that diviner vision
and understanding of life, of those
larger spiritual interpretations and
consolations which came by Jesus
Christ.   The history of much that
is called Christianity may be
largely the history of distrust and
fear, but when we return to the simplicity that is in Christ we return
to confidence and courage, to tranquillity and joy.   The true voice of
our religion is the voice of Jesus
to the trembling, storm-tossed disciples on the old Galilean sea, "Be
of good cheer, be not afraid."

The great trusts of religion
which find expression in the Bible
are the anticipations of what science and experience have been
disclosing and verifying.   The
confidence that all things are very
good in their purpose and end,
and that the universe is essentially beneficent in all its operations though it transcends exact
knowledge, is yet justified by it.
An earlier science, by its revela-

tion of the severe side of nature,
may have turned some minds away
from faith, but later and truer
knowledge is restoring religious
conviction by quickening and in-
creasing our confidence in the
nature and course of things. The
more we search and the more we
study the relation of each part to
the whole, and of the whole to
each, the more do we see that
what we call evil is but good
in the making. There is no trace
of curse or caprice anywhere.
Everywhere we see wisdom and
goodness—one purpose, one law,
one power, one God throughout
the universe. At the root of all
the seeming hardness and severity
of nature there is mercy and faithfulness. We live in a world that
is under God's love and blessing,
not "under God's wrath and
curse." The universe is what
Jesus Christ said it was, "My
Father's house."

We cannot hide from ourselves

the dark side of human life, and we do not want a faith which does not fully recognise it; but when we study the drift and tendency of things God becomes His own interpreter. God and good are perceived to be one, and our human world is seen to be moving through such processes as moral growth requires toward harmony with good. "If God made this world," says one of our philosophical pessimists, "I should not like to be God; its woes would break my heart." But the world is not made; it is only in the process of making. The week of creation is a long week. "Rest in the Lord, wait patiently for Him." The end will explain and vindicate both the length and severity of the process. God's world, when finished, will be far better than our best thought of what a world might and ought to be. A careful study of the past affords sufficient justification for our largest expectations as to the coming years. The movement is ever toward good. The centuries grow juster, more merciful, more peaceful.

> Step by step since time began,
> We see the steady gain of man.

We may, indeed, trust life as meaning our good. It may be difficult to understand things when we are in the midst of them; but by slow stages the knowledge dawns on every thoughtful and faithful man that life is underlaid with beneficent purpose. The conditions may be hard, but character can only be formed through struggle; and the formation or training of character is the justification and explanation of the discipline of our days. We grow by what seems to thwart us; defeats are sometimes the best victories, and adversities and griefs the very conditions of fulfilling the noblest prophecy of life.

The words, "I will trust and not be afraid," describe what ought to be our attitude toward God in all our personal and immediate relations to Him. God ought not to be the object of any base fear; He is the refuge from all such fear. "What time I am afraid I will trust in Thee." To see God as He is revealed in Jesus Christ is to trust Him and to be at rest in Him. We are much, it is true, that we ought not to be, and little that we ought to be. We need no arguments to convince us that we are weak and sinful. We have terrible inward evidence of transgression and failure. But it is only the heart without faith and hope that wears itself out in regrets and fears. We who profess to believe in the Eternal Love revealed in the character and Cross of Jesus Christ need not have tormenting memories and forebodings as our companions in the coming days.

The most central truth of our
religion is just the helpfulness—
the everlasting helpfulness of God.
This—when we put aside all those
accretions which have gathered
about it in its passage through
the thoughts of men—this is the
message of Jesus Christ to mankind, what lies at the heart of His
Gospel,—there is mercy for all,
love for all, hope for all, help for
all in God. And He, indeed, is
the Saviour of the world, our
Saviour from all ignorant and
guilty fears, who can inspire us
with this triumphant confidence,
this enthusiasm of faith in Eternal
Goodness and Mercy. We do not
require to be protected and delivered from God; He is our
Protector and Deliverer. His
character is the ultimate ground
of human trust.

The attitude of trust ought to
be our attitude toward the mysterious future. It is natural to
desire some clear and authentic

assurance concerning the life that
lies on the other side of death. A
longing to pierce the darkness
comes at times to all who have
loved and lost. When knowledge
fails superstition often comes in,
and men and women become the
victims of their own credulous
fancies and fears. But it is well
that we do not know. In drawing
a veil over to-morrow God is not
dealing with us as an austere and
capricious Master, but as a Father
who pities His children and knows
what they can bear, and what is
best for the healthy movement
and progress of their life. We
must leave the future to trust and
hope. Yet it is not altogether a
matter of uncertainty. The
Divine Goodness is an everlasting
certainty. God will be in the
future what He is in the present.
He rules all the worlds with equal
justice and equal love. Not alone
for these brief and troubled
mortal years is He our Father

and Saviour, but for ever. His
laws will never play false with us ;
His mercy will never fail us.   In
this life we are in the hollow of
His hand, and death only casts us
more entirely into His righteous
and gracious power.   Let us put
aside all tormenting fears and
anxieties as to what God may
be or do to us hereafter.   Outside of ourselves the universe
holds nothing that we need
dread.   Faith is not perfect till
it attains to this calm acceptance
of the universe ; this calm confidence · towards the seen and the
unseen; this calm sense of the
unknown as being as trustworthy as
the known.   Whatever may be the
mystery of the future, the most
truly Christian disposition is the
most trustful and hopeful disposition.   In a universe over which
such a God reigns as Jesus Christ
revealed there is surely nothing
too good to be true.   The reality
will be better than our best

thought, and fairer than our fairest dream. Here and hereafter we must reap what we sow, yet the great moral reality which Scripture calls "the wrath of God" is but the severity of the Divine Goodness after all. In all, and through all the Father is redeeming and educating His children. From His love no soul is ever outcast; to His love no soul is ever lost.

> And so, beside the silent sea,
> I wait the muffled oar;
> No harm from Him can come to me
> On ocean or on shore.

"Trust in the Lord"—*there is our attitude toward the Unknown and the Unknowable.* The Unknown and the Unknowable may be, and ought to be trusted. With one of our modern seers we surely can say, "All I have seen bids me trust the Creator for all I have not seen."

"Do good"—*there is our duty in the region of the Known,* in the

realm of human relation and cir-
cumstance, in the realm of daily
life. We cannot choose our life,
but we can choose the way we shall
live it. We can resolve and strive
whatever betides, to be good and
to do good, ever to be loyal to the
truest and best we know, and thus
to compel the rapidly vanishing
days to leave a blessing behind.
We can subdue the temper which
troubles and makes unlovely our life
with others. We can put out of our
business everything which cannot
bear the searching scrutiny of the
righteous Lord and Brother of men.
So near is this, and so simple is
the beginning of the Christian
life.   So near as this and so
simple is the way out of per-
plexity and doubt toward certainty
and peace.

Let us do good and trust in the
Lord. Let us speak and act the
truth, confident in the ultimate
victory of truth. Let us do the
right, even against every apparent

interest, assured that it can never be our real interest to set ourselves at variance with the Divine law. The man utterly loyal to truth and right in all his strivings and in all the critical hours of his life, is the man who has the most real faith in God. Whatever happens, it must ever in this world and in all the worlds be well with him. The universe is in league with truth and righteousness of life. To be moving towards good is to have directly on our side the power that is making and ruling the world for good, and to have become active partakers in the Divine triumph over evil.

O, Thou from whom we come and to whom we go, the Beginning of our days, the End of our mortal journey and the Home of our souls! perfect that within us which concerneth us. Give us to discern the purpose for which Thou hast sent us here. Give us the power to do

the work which Thou hast set for
us to do. Keep us from following
what is false and vain and un-
profitable. Reconcile us to Thy
will. Help us to obey as Thy
Belovéd Son obeyed; and to trust
in God and love man even as He
trusted and loved. Take out of
our hearts all suspicion and fear,
and let our honest doubts ripen
into larger and richer trusts.
Make us calm and strong in the
faith that Thou art always near,
that our little lives are part of
Thine, and that in this world and
in every world the Eternal God is
our Refuge, and underneath us are
the Everlasting Arms. We pray
in His name who made known
Thy gracious purposes to mankind.
Amen.

www.ingramcontent.com/pod-product-compliance
Lightning Source LLC
Chambersburg PA
CBHW030556270326
41927CB00007B/938